LEADING WOMEN

Beyoncé

Entertainment
Industry
Icon

KATIE GRIFFITHS

Cavendish
Square

New York

Published in 2018 by Cavendish Square Publishing, LLC
243 5th Avenue, Suite 136, New York, NY 10016

Website: cavendishsq.com

This publication represents the opinions and views of the author based on his or her personal
experience, knowledge, and research. The information in this book serves as a general guide only.
The author and publisher have used their best efforts in preparing this book and disclaim
liability rising directly or indirectly from the use and application of this book.

CPSIA Compliance Information: Batch #CS17CSQ

All websites were available and accurate when this book was sent to press.

Library of Congress Cataloging-in-Publication Data

Names: Griffiths, Katie.
Title: Beyoncé : entertainment industry icon / Katie Griffiths.Description: New York : Cavendish
Square Publishing, [2018] | Series: Leading women |
Includes bibliographical references and index.
Identifiers: LCCN 2016053727 (print) | LCCN 2016054488 (ebook) |
ISBN 9781502627056 (library bound) | ISBN 9781502627063 (E-book)
Subjects: LCSH: Beyoncé, 1981---Juvenile literature. |
Singers--United States--Biography--Juvenile literature. |
Rhythm and blues musicians--United States--Biography--Juvenile literature. |
Classification: LCC ML3930.K66 G75 2017 (print) | LCC ML3930.K66 (ebook) |
DDC 782.42164092 [B] --dc23
LC record available at https://lccn.loc.gov/2016053727

Editorial Director: David McNamara
Editor: Tracey Maciejewski
Copy Editor: Nathan Heidelberger
Associate Art Director: Amy Greenan
Designer: Lindsay Auten
Production Coordinator: Karol Szymczuk
Photo Research: J8 Media

Printed in the United States of America

CONTENTS

CHAPTER ONE

About a Girl

I n 2015, *Forbes* magazine listed Beyoncé Knowles as the most powerful woman in the entertainment industry. For most, this did not come as a surprise. From her music career, to her self-**branding**, to her impassioned political activism, Beyoncé has long been a source of **inspiration** for millions around the world. Since her first break into the spotlight with the group Destiny's Child, Beyoncé has risen to become an icon of female power, talent, and **creativity**. Her effortless style and business savvy make it easy to believe that the singer and entrepreneur has always been the strong and

Beyoncé accepts the award for Video of the Year at the 2016 MTV Video Music Awards.

empowered role model presented to the world today. But this was not always so. A key part of understanding how Beyoncé became the leader she is now is a knowledge of her family background and the struggles she went through, in both her personal and professional life. It was through such support and such trials that Beyoncé was to truly become a force of nature.

A Name and a Legacy

On September 4, 1981, Beyoncé Giselle Knowles was born to Tina and Mathew Knowles at Park Plaza Hospital in Houston, Texas. Her parents had agreed that Tina would pick her first name, and Mathew her second. Worried that her maiden name, Beyincé, would die out, Tina decided to name her first child Beyoncé as a tribute to her own family. It was not the last time that the importance and value of honoring one's family would be impressed upon Beyoncé, as it had been impressed upon her mother.

Beyoncé's parents grew up with very different ideals and family structures. Her mother, Celestine "Tina" Beyincé, was the youngest of seven children. The family was of Louisiana **Creole** descent with a mix of African, Spanish, French, and Native American heritage. Through her mother's side, Beyoncé is a descendant of Joseph Broussard, a leader of the Acadian people in Acadia, which later became the Canadian provinces of Nova Scotia, Prince Edward Island, and New Brunswick. Tina's parents were both French-speaking Creoles. Her mother, Agnez DeRouen, was a talented and highly sought after self-taught seamstress with a bevy of wealthy clientele. She was known for her dramatic and flamboyant designs, a creative trait that would be passed on to Tina and later Beyoncé herself. Tina's father, Lumis Beyincé, was also known locally for his tailored and elegant appearance. It was said that despite the fact he worked as a laborer, most people in their neighborhood believed him to be a scholar due to his fine suits. Though Tina loved both of her parents, her mother held a very special place as Tina grew older. In interviews, Tina often said how much she wanted to emulate her mother and follow her advice. This feeling would later impact her relationship with her own daughters. In one interview, Tina said, "I've always hoped my daughters would feel the same way about me."[1] It was her mother that would also be the formation for Tina's views on family—specifically that you never walked away from family. This would later massively impact her relationships with both her daughters and her husband.

As a teen, Tina was a creative, sociable person. An active member of the church and its choir, she would later be in her own girl group, the Veltones, where she would design her own costumes with the help of her mother, Agnez.

Beyoncé's father, on the other hand, came from a very different kind of family, despite similarly being one of seven children. The Knowles family was more independent and self-sufficient. Whereas Tina learned the value of togetherness from her parents, Mathew learned a different set of values. Mathew was born in the small city of Gadsden, Alabama, near Birmingham. His parents were both African American. His mother, Lue Helen, worked as a maid for a white family, but it was Mathew's father who would have the greatest impact on the man he would become. Matthew (two t's) Knowles was a large man, both in size and personality. His nickname among his coworkers was "Big Boy" or "Big Mack." He was famous locally for his activities as a fireman, able to move the heavy and unwieldy water hoses that other professional firemen couldn't lift. He was a naturally skilled entrepreneur, always looking for new ways to make money. This **attitude** in particular would influence his son Mathew's personality in later life. In Mathew's own words, "My people didn't have a lot of money … but they had drive and ambition, a strong work ethic, and a business savvy which I recognized at an early age and began to emulate."[2]

Money was a constant worry in the Knowles household as Mathew grew older. His mother always seemed to be criticizing his father for not earning enough, and Mathew had strong memories of his father extolling the importance of good credit.

Like Tina, Mathew was a creative personality, though this manifested in different ways. As well as being in his own boy band for a while, Mathew was also a keen

Beyoncé with father Mathew, sister Solange, and mother Tina

basketball player and joined his high-school team. As he moved into the working world, he soon became notorious both for his hardworking ethos and his demanding attitude of others. By 1981, the year of Beyoncé's birth, this drive had resulted in Mathew driving a Jaguar XJ6 car and earning a six-figure income. This was a level of success quite unheard of for a black salesman in the 1980s.

In 1986, a few years after she was born, Beyoncé was joined by her sister, Solange. Sharing her sister's love of music, Solange would later follow Beyoncé into the music industry and forge a career of her own.

A Rocky Start

Despite the birth of a new baby, Tina and Mathew's home life took a severe hit during the first months of Beyoncé's life. Due to personal issues, Mathew was absent from the family home and Tina was left without financial security and with a newborn to raise. By this time, her own mother had passed away, and Tina needed to find a way to care for her new baby and to gain back the financial stability she had lost. In the end, she took Beyoncé to stay with her paternal grandmother, Lue Helen, and worked to make her hair salon business into a success. After roughly six months, Mathew returned to the family home and Beyoncé was brought back from her grandparents' house. But from this moment on, Tina was established as an independent businesswoman and was determined never to be financially dependent on a man again.

Bullies and a New Beyoncé

Despite the commanding stage presence she now brings to her public events, Beyoncé was extremely shy as a young child and had few friends. Before moving to homeschooling in the ninth grade, she attended public schools and often found herself the target of bullies.

Beyoncé has often spoken about the hate she used to receive for her light hair and skin. Her mother, Tina, has previously spoken out on the issue of skin color in black communities. Specifically she noted the awful impact on young men and women who fall into either the "lighter than average" or "darker than average" category within a certain community and the incidents of bullying that can occur. Beyoncé also found that her own name was a source of ridicule for sounding too exotic. In an interview, she recalled: "I hated my name when I was a kid. It was just something else for them to use against me." The taunting began a vicious cycle that exacerbated Beyoncé's natural shyness. "I couldn't win," she recalled, "I was bashful because the kids picked on me. And I was then picked on because I was bashful." Eventually, her parents decided to sign the young girl up for a dance class, as Tina told *Essence* magazine, "to make friends more than anything else."[3] Both Tina and Mathew hoped that the classes would help give Beyoncé more self-esteem.

It was during these classes that Beyoncé's gift for singing was first seriously recognized. During a class, instructor Darlene Johnson began humming a song, and Beyoncé finished it, able to hit the very high notes despite her young age. At the class's next show, Beyoncé performed in public for the first time. Both her parents were in the audience. The experience would have a dramatic effect on the young girl:

It was the first time I have ever walked onstage in front of an audience. I looked into the crowd and saw teachers, classmates, and parents ... Then I opened my mouth and started to sing. My parents were shocked. I can still see the looks on their faces. I'm not sure where I found the courage. All I know is that I felt at home on that stage, more so than anywhere else. I saw my parents stand up and clap after I sang. I knew they were very proud of me ... From that moment on, I decided that all the world would be a stage—chairs, tables, the kitchen countertop ... That's how I expressed myself—through music. I only felt comfortable when I was singing or dancing. My personality would totally change. It's still true today. Normally, I keep to myself, and you wouldn't even know if I was in the same room. But when I'm in performance mode, I become a totally different person.[4]

Indeed, Beyoncé dove straight into performance. At the age of seven, she won her first competition by participating in a school talent show, singing John Lennon's "Imagine" and beating her fifteen- and sixteen-year-old competitors.

Hoping to encourage her daughter's talent and new **confidence**, Tina began enrolling Beyoncé in local beauty pageants. She was less interested in the beauty segments and more concerned with finding her daughter a space to practice her singing in public. Beyoncé would learn a lot during her time in such pageants, including the value of healthy competition and how to improve your own performance by watching the competitors. However, she truly hated the beauty portion of such shows and was left with a lot of unresolved feelings that would later be explored in her song "Pretty Hurts." By this time, her father had begun to get more involved in Beyoncé's talent and aspirations, encouraging her to do more pageants and to work to improve her abilities.

Girls Tyme

In 1990 Beyoncé auditioned for and won a place in an all-girl entertainment group. The lineup included Támar Davies, Nikki and Nina Taylor, LaTavia Roberson, and Beyoncé's childhood friend Kelly Rowland. The group was named Girls Tyme, and they began life by dancing and rapping on talent shows in Houston. Eventually they came to the attention of West Coast R&B producer Arne Frager. After flying to Houston to meet the girls in person, he brought the group back to his Northern California operation, The Plant Recording Studios. Frager attempted to land the girls a major record deal by debuting them on *Star Search*, the biggest national talent competition on television at the time. However, the group lost the competition, and with it, Frager's plans for a record deal.

After the group's defeat, Mathew voluntarily dedicated himself to managing the group. The change was both drastic and intense. He cut the original lineup of Girls Tyme from six to four, removing Davis and the Taylor sisters, and bringing in LeToya Luckett in 1993.

Along with singing in church, the girls would practice routines in their backyards and at Tina's salon. Customers from the salon would give feedback on their routines and sometimes the girls would collect tips. Later they moved to performing regularly at local gigs. During the summer months, Mathew set up a band boot camp where the group trained for long hours to improve their singing and dancing. Soon they were performing as a warm-up act for established R&B groups, such as SWV, Dru Hill, and Immature. Tina designed the group's matching outfits. They changed band names, experimenting with Somethin' Fresh, Cliché, The Dolls, and Destiny. Eventually they settled on the name Destiny's Child, a reference taken from the biblical Book of Isaiah.

Becoming a Leader

It's clear to see that Beyoncé's upbringing dramatically impacted the person she became. Her history shows significant points where her work ethic and personality were shaped by the people and circumstances around her. Her maternal legacy of strong, creative women, in the forms of grandmother Agnez and mother Tina, clearly showed the young Beyoncé the importance of self-respect and creativity. Agnez passed much advice to Tina as she was growing up: "Never give yourself one hundred percent to any man. Always keep something for yourself … No man needs that much control … Don't give away your power … Live your own life … Find something to do that's your own"[5] This advice would go on to show itself time and time again in Beyoncé's use of media and the sociopolitical messages of her music.

The parental support Beyoncé received as a child to chase her dream, as well as the huge sacrifices both Tina and Mathew made in order to give her the necessary opportunities, helped to build Beyoncé's own sense of self-esteem. Her experience of beauty pageants opened her eyes to the dangerous pressures placed on women and girls to look and act in certain ways, which would later play out in her activism on behalf of women. Similarly, the racism that she experienced and that she saw her father experience would also affect her future political activism through music. As she once noted: "My father was part of the first generation of black men that attended an all-white school … and he has grown up with a lot of trauma from those experiences. I feel that, now, I can sing for his pain … and I can sing for my grandparents' pain as well."[6] This desire to give a voice to people that society had failed would heavily inform her style of leadership in later years.

Beyoncé and Beauty Pageants

It is not unusual for child stars to feel as if they lost or never fully experienced their childhoods. In fact, it is one of the most common complaints of entertainers who became famous at a young age. Beyoncé did not become famous until she was sixteen. However, she did experience this feeling to an extent due to her time in beauty pageants. What her mother had started as an exercise in growing Beyoncé's confidence was soon taken over by her father, who saw huge potential in how far Beyoncé could go and wanted to push her further. This is not to say that Beyoncé was forced into pageants. It has been noted by friends and family in several biographies of the singer that once her parents opened the possibility of pageants to her, Beyoncé's competitive side most definitely shone. However, her time competing left the singer with unresolved feelings that would not be fully addressed for many years. In one interview, she noted:

> Getting all dolled up was not for me at that age … I was too self-conscious and didn't feel like I was as pretty as the other girls.[7]

Her value was questioned again and again and put a huge amount of pressure on Beyoncé to keep proving herself. Biographer J. Randy Taraborrelli explains:

> Those years of putting herself forth for harsh judgment and heavy scrutiny—she would later look back and feel a certain amount of discontentment. Was she talented enough? It was a question constantly drummed into her head just by virtue of the competitive venue in which she found herself.[8]

CHAPTER TWO

Ten Thousand Hours

I t is a commonly held belief among performance experts that if a person wants to become a master of something, he or she must complete ten thousand hours of practice. If this is true, then it was certainly Beyoncé's training with Girls Tyme, and later Destiny's Child, that honed her skills. Her early success with Destiny's Child is where Beyoncé first encountered true stardom and global

Beyoncé's trip to the top with band Destiny's Child was not an easy journey.

recognition. It was this period that taught her how to deal with negative media attention and improved her songwriting and performance capabilities. It gave her time to both practice her craft and develop as an artist. It is arguable that it was this time of growth that would later give her such an edge over her contemporaries in the music industry.

Destiny Begun

After her father took over the group's management in 1995, there were big changes. Mathew resigned from his job in order to devote himself full time to training the girls. This effectively cut the family's income in half, and as a result, her parents were forced to move into separate apartments. As part of his plan to transform Destiny's Child into a success, Mathew introduced an intense training program for the group and continued booking gigs for them as an opening act for established R&B groups. They also auditioned for and were eventually signed to Elektra Records, moving to Atlanta Records briefly to work on their first recording.

In 1996 things truly began moving for the group. Mathew helped to negotiate a record deal with Columbia Records, who signed the girls the same year. The group had already been working on several tracks with producer D'wayne Wiggins, including the song "Killing Time." The label was so enthusiastic about the track that they had it included in the soundtrack to the 1997 film *Men in Black*, starring Will Smith and Tommy Lee Jones.

Destiny's Child released their self-titled debut album on February 17, 1998. Still at the beginning of her career, Beyoncé wrote only three of the thirteen songs on the album. However, she was already showing interest in issues geared toward female experiences. In her biography of the singer, writer Janice Arenofsky notes:

> *Despite Beyoncé's relative inexperience with the opposite sex, she zeroed in on issues that resonated with many women and young girls. The source of many of her ideas was eavesdropping on conversations in Headliners Hair Salon in Houston.*[1]

Exploring relationships through a lens of feminism, power balances, and emotional **honesty** would continue to be a source of inspiration for Beyoncé for the rest of her career.

The album *Destiny's Child* reached number sixty-seven in the *Billboard* 200 chart and number fourteen in the *Billboard* Top R&B/Hip-Hop Albums chart. It sold over one million copies in the United States, thus earning platinum certification by the Recording Industry Association of America (RIAA).

Its most popular track, "No, No, No," was remixed by music producer Wyclef Jean. His influence changed the track from a slow, soulful melody to a faster, more dance-friendly single. It eventually reached number one on the *Billboard* Hot R&B/Hip-Hop Singles and Tracks chart and number three on the *Billboard* Hot 100 chart. Jean later stated that he wanted to help produce the album due to the group's obvious potential: "In the line of work we are in, you can see who's gonna blow and who's not gonna blow." He particularly noted Beyoncé and Kelly Rowland's "humility and laid-back attitude," and he believed that "people with that mindset achieved long-term success in the entertainment industry."[2] Their success began almost immediately, with Destiny's Child gathering three Soul Train Lady of Soul Awards, including Best New Artist for "No, No, No."

Growing Pains

Destiny's Child quickly reentered the studio to begin work on their next album, bringing in established producers such as Kevin "She'kspere" Briggs and Rodney Jerkins. Titled *The Writing's on the Wall*, the album dropped on July 27, 1999, and eventually became their breakthrough piece, launching the group onto **mainstream** media. The group's style had matured, and Beyoncé herself had gained more creative control. The key message of the album was to encourage women to be strong and independent from their boyfriends, husbands, and parents. Tracks such as "Say My Name," a song where a cheating boyfriend is called out, and "Bills, Bills, Bills," a song about dropping a lover who is living off his girlfriend's paycheck, spurred album sales and introduced their music to a wider audience. "Say My Name" alone topped the *Billboard* Hot 100 charts for three consecutive

The final Destiny's Child lineup: Kelly Rowland, Beyoncé Knowles, and
Michelle Williams

weeks. By the end of the year, *The Writing's on the Wall*
had sold more than eleven million copies worldwide and
was one of the top-selling albums of 2000.

Yet, despite the group's growing profile, among its
members, not all was well. Between late 1999 and early
2000, internal management issues led to members Luckett
and Roberson leaving the band. They were replaced with
Michelle Williams, a former backup singer to R&B star
Monica, and Farrah Franklin, an aspiring singer-actress.

Beyoncé began to learn the hard way how easily the
media could turn. Spurred on by the animosity of the lawsuit

23

Luckett and Roberson brought against manager Mathew Knowles, Beyoncé became a target of blame for the breakup of the band. She also split from her long-term boyfriend during this period. Still only nineteen, she developed a severe depression which would last for the next two years. At its worst, she would lock herself in her bedroom for days and refuse to eat anything. The singer would later reveal how she struggled to speak about her depression at the time. Destiny's Child had just won their first Grammy, and Beyoncé was afraid no one would take her seriously. In the end, it was her mother's support and strength that helped her to fight it. As one biographer writes:

The legal fight also stripped Beyoncé of her **naïveté***, which probably did her a favor. In the beginning, her response to criticism from fans and audiences was to lead everyone in prayer, but as she matured, she became more thick-skinned and self-protective.*[3]

This attitude would later become a big part of her leadership style and the **persona** she presented to the world.

In March 2000, Farrah Franklin also left the group, giving as reasons the negativity caused by the departure of Luckett and Roberson, and the lack of control she had in the group's decision making. However, it was also claimed that Franklin continually missed appointments and was unable or unwilling to give the level of **commitment** the group required. Yet, despite—

or perhaps because of—the controversy surrounding Destiny's Child, the group's success continued to grow, and they began opening for acts such as Britney Spears and Christina Aguilera.

Survivors

Now refined to a trio, Destiny's Child began their new life with the release of a theme song for the 2000 film *Charlie's Angels*. Debuted in October of the same year, "Independent Women Part 1" was an instant feminist anthem and spent eleven consecutive weeks atop the *Billboard* Hot 100, from November 2000 to January 2001. It was the longest-running number-one single of Destiny Child's career. The track boosted sales of the original soundtrack album to 1.5 million by 2001. The group also received numerous awards, including winning *Soul Train's* Sammy David Jr. Entertainer of the Year Award in 2001 and the *Billboard's* Artist of the Year Award in both 2000 and 2001.

Despite their growing fame, the group continued to be hounded by criticism and speculation of poor group dynamics. One radio DJ, in particular, compared Destiny's Child to the television show *Survivor*: "You had to guess which member would be out next!"[4] Hurt and angered by the gossip, Beyoncé channeled her feelings into the trio's third album and specifically into the title track, "Survivor."

From the mid-2000s to early 2001, Destiny's Child worked on writing and recording their third album. Beyoncé's creative sway grew further, and she was credited as a writer and producer on almost every song. *Survivor* hit stores in the spring and entered straight into the *Billboard* 200 charts at number one. It sold over 663,000 in its first week. The first three released singles, "Independent Women Part 1," "Survivor," and "Bootylicious," charted within the top three in the United States, and the first two singles were consecutive number ones in the United Kingdom. The album itself was certified four-time platinum. By the end of 2001, the trio had picked up two Grammy Awards and an American Music Award.

The early 2000s also saw the girls' first **forays** into solo work. While Beyoncé worked on her first solo musical work, the other two members explored their own interests. In 2002, Williams released her solo album *Heart to Yours*, a contemporary gospel collection which reached the number-one position in the *Billboard* Top Gospel chart. Meanwhile, Rowland collaborated with hip-hop artist Nelly on the single "Dilemma." The track became a worldwide hit, earning Rowland a Grammy and transforming her into the group's first member to achieve a solo number-one single. She soon followed this up with the album *Simply Deep*.

Destiny Fulfilled

After a three-year hiatus, the trio reunited to record their fourth album, *Destiny Fulfilled*. Designed with a grittier, more urban sound, the album showed the strides all three had taken in their musical maturity. Each member contributed to songwriting on the majority of songs, and all three were featured as executive producers alongside their manager. Though it did not top *Survivor*'s success, the album was still one of the best-selling albums of 2005 and sold over eight million copies worldwide.

To promote the album, Destiny's Child embarked on a worldwide tour called Destiny Fulfilled ... and Lovin' It, but on June 11, 2005, while performing at the Palau Sant Jordi in Barcelona, Spain, the group announced before sixteen thousand people their disbandment. The group later sent an official letter to MTV:

> *We have been working together as Destiny's Child since we were 9, and touring together since we were 14. After a lot of discussion and some deep soul searching, we realized that our current tour has given us the opportunity to leave Destiny's Child on a high note, united in our friendship and filled with an overwhelming gratitude for our music, our fans, and each other. After all these wonderful years working together, we realized that now is the time to pursue our personal goals and solo efforts in earnest ... No matter what happens, we will always love each other as friends and sisters and will always support each other as artists. We want to thank all of our fans for their incredible love and support and hope to see you all again as we continue fulfilling our destinies.[5]*

Desipte the announcement, the group continued with the American leg of their tour. They released an album of their greatest hits, *#1's*, on October 25, 2005. The collection revisited their well-known anthems, such as "Survivor" and "Bootylicious," and also included three brand-new tracks. Destiny's Child gave their farewell performance at the 2006 NBA All-Star Game in Houston, Texas. The following March, they were inducted into the Hollywood Walk of Fame.

Learning a Lifestyle

Beyoncé learned a great deal from her time with Destiny's Child. The group gave her a space to develop her artistic abilities and performance style, and it gave her real-world insight into how to operate within the entertainment industry. In addition, it was this period that first introduced her to media management. She learned not only how to deal with negative media attention and criticism but also how to split her life into the public and the private, keeping a space for herself that the media would never have access to. As an artistic leader, she gained the skills and experience to craft music that would deliver not only a great dance track but also messages that could be political or spiritual, depending on her mood. As a sociopolitical leader, Beyoncé found in Destiny's Child a vehicle to test out feminist messages that challenged contemporary attitudes of dating and female roles in society.

As Beyoncé moved into her solo career, she was primed to use all her experiences to build a media empire.

Keep It in the Family

Beyoncé's sister, Solange Piaget Knowles, was born on June 24, 1986. From an early age, she too showed an interest in the arts, studying music and dance as a child. She made her initial debut as a singer at the tender age of five at a local amusement park. By nine, she was writing her own songs. Soon she was trying to persuade her parents to let her pursue a career in entertainment. Her parents, however, worried by her young age, initially advised her to wait until she was older to decide. Moving into her teenage years, as she watched Beyoncé's career flourish, she became more certain that the music industry was her destiny too. At fifteen, she replaced a missing dancer during a Destiny's Child tour and performed onstage with Beyoncé and her groupmates. She did several stints as a backup singer and dancer for them until she was eventually signed to her father's record label, Music World. Mathew was also Solange's manager at this time. In 2002, sixteen-year-old Solange released her debut solo album, *Solo Star*.

As well as creating her own music, Solange worked on songs for other artists. She wrote a number of tracks for the now-solo Destiny's Child stars. This included the track "Alone" on Rowland's album *Simply Deep* and the singles "Upgrade U" and "Get Me Bodied" for Beyoncé's 2006 album *B'Day*. In 2008, she released her second studio album, *Sol-Angel and the Hadley St. Dreams*. In 2013, Solange launched her own record label, Saint Records, to release her future music projects. Her third album, titled *A Seat at the Table*, was released in September 2016.

CHAPTER THREE

B'Day

After being part of a group since age nine, Beyoncé now looked to break out as a solo artist. Her time with Destiny's Child had trained her to be a solid performer, and while the public often spoke about her "inevitable" solo career, she still had a lot to prove—both to herself and her critics. She worked hard to redefine herself and her image to fans. She moved into acting, took greater and greater control of her music and her management, and matured significantly as an artist.

Breaking Out

In 2002, Beyoncé's first project as an individual came in the form of a film, not a record. Comedian Mike Myers was producing the third movie in his Austin

Beyoncé in Manchester, England, on the opening night of her Dangerously in Love world tour

Powers series, a set of comic spoofs of 1960s spy films, and Beyoncé was cast in the role of Foxxy Cleopatra. This character was in itself a parody of crime-fighting African American heroines from the 1970s. Her name was a combination of Foxy Brown and Cleopatra Jones, two real characters from famous crime films of the era. Working in unfamiliar territory was a nerve-racking experience for Beyoncé. She didn't understand the industry **jargon** and felt uncomfortable at the audition. In the Destiny's Child biography *Soul Survivors*, Beyoncé reveals that it was her mother that helped her once again:

> *I was scared that I was going to say the wrong thing and ruin it, so I thought it would be best if I listened and didn't say much. My mom did all the talking—fortunately, she's a real charmer, and she did everything but read my lines for me!* [1]

Despite the learning curve, the film was a success, and her performance was praised by critics and fans alike.

In October of the same year, she was featured on rapper Jay Z's "'03 Bonnie & Clyde." She sang the chorus and bridge, and in the accompanying music video the two played updated versions of the notorious 1930s bank robber couple Bonnie Parker and Clyde Barrow. The track peaked at number four on the *Billboard* Hot 100 chart. The song also marked the beginning of the pair's relationship. However, the high value that Beyoncé placed on privacy meant that she refused to publicly speak about this relationship for years afterward.

"'03 Bonnie & Clyde" was just the start of Beyoncé and Jay Z's professional and personal relationship.

The Debut

Dangerously in Love dropped in June 2003. This was Beyoncé's long-awaited debut solo album, and it did not disappoint. In its first week, it sold 317,000 copies. Its lead single, "Crazy in Love," featuring Jay Z, became the singer's first solo number one. Other tracks were also extremely successful, with "Baby Boy" hitting number one in the US charts, and singles "Me, Myself and I" and "Naughty Girl" both reaching the top five. The album immediately established her solo reputation around the world and earned her five Grammy Awards, including Best Contemporary Album and Best Female R&B Vocal Performance.

Soon after, Beyoncé was back in the studio to record her final album with Destiny's Child. In June 2005, during their tour, the group announced their plans to disband. Beyoncé soon began working on a follow-up solo album, with the added pressure of *Dangerously in Love*'s success driving her to improve on her previous work.

Her second album, *B'Day*, a play on both her name and the word "birthday," was released on September 4, 2006, to coincide with the singer's twenty-fifth birthday. It sold over 541,000 copies in its first week and went straight to number one in the *Billboard* 200 album charts, becoming Beyoncé's second consecutive number-one album. Its most noticeable hits included "Déjà Vu" and "Beautiful Liar," but undoubtedly its biggest success was the track "Irreplaceable." With its catchy hook of "To the left, to the left," the song was about a woman who discovers her boyfriend is cheating on her and, rather than drowning in self-pity, brushes it off and promptly kicks him out. When he retorts that she is a "fool" and she will never "find a man like [him]," she swiftly reminds her lover that he is not "irreplaceable." The single came out in November and went straight to number one, staying there for ten weeks. The official music video introduced the world to Beyoncé's new band, which consisted only of women and was named Suga Mama. She would play with them during live concerts for the next several years. This was simply another step in her established path of female support and power. Now that she was a solo artist with almost complete creative control, she was able to achieve practical results—namely replacing an all-male band with an all-female one. This step highlighted the hypocrisy that having an all-female band could still cause a double take while having an all-male band was viewed as normal.

During this period, Beyoncé continued to work on her acting career as well. In 2006, she starred in the remake of comedy classic *The Pink Panther*. She played singer Xania, girlfriend of a French soccer coach whose death begins the plot. She released the song "Check on It" as part of the official soundtrack. Though the movie was **panned** by critics, it did well commercially and gave Beyoncé further experience of working on a film set.

Beyoncé's first serious acting role came quickly on the heels of *The Pink Panther*, with a leading part in *Dreamgirls*. This was a film version of the 1981 Broadway musical loosely based on the famous 1960s girl group the Supremes. Beyoncé played Deena, a soft-spoken backup singer who rises to become the group's front woman. The film dealt with the difficulties of becoming a success and the inherent racism within the 1960s music industry. The role's depth gave Beyoncé the chance to show greater skill and **emotional range** than her previous film work. It became a huge success, acclaimed by both fans and critics, grossing $154 million internationally.

Beyoncé as Deena Jones in the 2006 film *Dreamgirls*

Not one to slack, Beyoncé shot *Dreamgirls* alongside her songwriting for *B'Day* and promotion of mother-daughter fashion project the House of Deréon, a fashion house set up in memory of Beyoncé's grandmother with designs by her mother Tina. Beyoncé ended the year on a high, winning the Grammy for Best Contemporary R&B Album for *B'Day*.

Enter Sasha Fierce

On October 22, 2008, during a new album listening party, Beyoncé publicly revealed that she had secretly married Jay Z, back in April of that year. But this was not the only news she had to introduce. The new album was Beyoncé's third, and it revealed another important person in the singer's life, her alter ego Sasha Fierce. In interviews, she later explained that Sasha Fierce had been invented during the making of her 2003 single "Crazy in Love."

I have someone else that takes over when it's time for me to work and when I'm on stage, this alter ego that I've created that kind of protects me and who I really am. That's why half the record ... is about who I am underneath all the make-up, underneath the lights, and underneath all the exciting star drama. And Sasha Fierce is the fun, more sensual, more aggressive, more outspoken, and more glamorous side that comes out when I'm working and when I'm on stage. The double album allows me to take more risks and really step out of myself, or shall I say, step more into myself, and reveal a side of me that only people who know me see.[2]

Beyoncé performs to a packed arena in Melbourne, Australia, on her
I Am ... tour.

Released in November and titled *I Am ... Sasha Fierce*, the album was a dual set designed to show two distinct sides of Beyoncé's personality. As one critic put it:

> If B'Day *had been Beyonce's hurried, rough-edges-showing work, then* I Am ... Sasha Fierce *was painstakingly put together. The first disc,* I Am ... *provided a showcase for her balladry; but on it, she explored different musical* **approaches**, *including British indie and folk music. Sasha Fierce would reinforce her penchant for up-tempo grooves.*[3]

Beyoncé was trying to show herself as a **multidimensional** artist, exploring female experiences though two personas—one powerful, confident, and self-assured, and the other more vulnerable but also more human. This was reflected in her mix of songs, from the infectious dance smash "Single Ladies (Put a Ring on It)" to the more soulful and thoughtful melodies of "Halo" and "If I Were a Boy." The album sold 482,000 copies in its first week and debuted atop the *Billboard* 200 chart, giving Beyoncé her third consecutive number one album.

This time the singer created not just an album but a phenomenon. The track "Single Ladies (Put a Ring on It)" was an instant success, spawning parodies and copies around the world. The video website YouTube found itself flooded with versions of the "Single Ladies'" dance performed by everyone from the likes of Justin Timberlake to high-school students in talents shows all over the country. The *Toronto Star* called it the "first major dance craze of both the new millennium and the Internet."[4] Despite its relatively simple **concept**, the video became a classic and won several awards, including Best Video at the 2009 MTV Europe Music Awards. It was another anthem in her growing tradition of songs about women who had been mistreated by men but who refused to be diminished and instead flip the social script. The personas of Beyoncé's songs are, by and large, not rejected or somehow worth less because they are not appreciated by men. They move on and start again, stronger for the experience but not in any way soiled by it. They know their own worth is separate from a male estimation.

One particular example of Beyoncé's leadership behavior came at the 2009 MTV Video Music Awards. She was nominated for several awards, including Best Female Video. However, this award was won instead by country-pop singer Taylor Swift for "You Belong with Me." When Swift attempted to give her acceptance speech, Kanye West, a rapper and friend of Jay Z, rushed the stage and took her microphone. He then proceeded to tell Swift that in fact Beyoncé deserved the award as "Single Ladies" was "the greatest video of all time."[5] Swift was left speechless, West was booed by the audience, and cameras turned to look at Beyoncé in the audience, focusing on her shocked expression. Later, when Beyoncé was giving her own acceptance speech for Video of the Year, she took pains to rectify what had happened. "I remember being seventeen years old," she told the audience of musicians and critics, "… up for my first MTV award with Destiny's Child. And it was one of the most exciting moments of my life, so I would like for Taylor to come out and have her moment."[6] Swift was brought back out on stage and given time to complete her acceptance speech. She later praised Beyoncé for her grace and sensitivity, saying: "It was just so wonderful and so incredibly classy of her."

Though Beyoncé was not responsible for West's behavior, she also realized the power she had to change the outcome of the situation. Instead of ignoring what happened, or disclaiming any responsibility, she gave up a few minutes of spotlight so that an up-and-coming performer could be allowed her moment.

The Rise and Rise

After her performance as Deena in *Dreamgirls*, Beyoncé began to receive offers for more serious acting work. In 2008, she starred in the musical biopic *Cadillac Records*, playing the part of Etta James, a real-life blues singer. The film followed the rise of record company Chess Records, which produced famous blues artists such as Muddy Waters, Chuck Berry, and Howlin' Wolf. Her performance received high praise from critics, and she received several nominations for her portrayal of James. She would later even perform James's famous song "At Last" for President Barack Obama and his wife, Michelle, at their first inaugural ball.

Beyoncé continued to garner awards for her musical output. At the Fifty-Second Grammy Awards, she received ten nominations, including Album of the Year for *I Am … Sasha Fierce*. She tied with record-holder Lauryn Hill for most Grammy nominations in a single year by a female artist, before going on to win six of the awards—a record for a female artist.

As she moved into 2010, Beyoncé collaborated with eclectic singer-songwriter Lady Gaga on the single "Telephone." She sang vocals for the track and also

Beyoncé electrifies as Etta James in 2008 biopic *Cadillac Records*.

appeared in the *Pulp Fiction*–inspired video. The song topped the *Billboard* Pop Songs chart, becoming the sixth number-one single for both Beyoncé and Gaga. The track also placed them in a tied position with Mariah Carey for most number-one singles since the Nielson Top 40 Airplay Chart launched in 1992.

Hiatus

In January of 2010, Beyoncé announced to the world that she was taking a break from her music career to follow her mother's advice to "live life, to be inspired by things again."[7] As she explained to *Cosmopolitan* magazine:

> *I've worked since the age of 15 and never taken any time out. My life has always been about next, next, next and moving on. I just decided to stop. It's the best decision I've ever made.*[8]

Her break from the industry lasted nine months in total. She used this time to visit multiple European cities, the Great Wall of China, the Egyptian pyramids, Australia, and English music festivals such as Glastonbury. She also visited various museums and ballet performances.

It was during this time that she also took over control of her own management and parted with her father as business partners. The move was friendly, but Beyoncé had realized she was ready and willing to be solely responsible for her career and her image.

Setting Precedent

Just as her time with Destiny's Child planted seeds for her solo career, Beyoncé's first few years as a solo artist laid the groundwork for the sociopolitical interests that she would continue to use and refine in later years. These two key interests were activism and female empowerment.

Between 2002 and 2010, Beyoncé was primarily concerned with activism in the form of charity and aid relief. In September 2005, she and former Destiny's Child partner Kelly Rowland set up the Survivor Foundation with help from their families. Its mission was to help victims of Hurricane Katrina within their hometown of Houston, Texas. The foundation helped survivors find temporary housing. Beyoncé herself donated $250,000 to the fund. In 2007, during her The Beyoncé Experience tour, the singer conducted preconcert food donation drives during six major stops. This was done in conjunction with the pastor of her childhood church and the America's Second Harvest food bank. In 2008, Beyoncé's role in *Cadillac Records* saw her exploring the substance abuse issues of real-life blues singer Etta James. She would later donate her entire salary from the film to Phoenix House, an organization of rehabilitation centers around the country. Before taking her career break in 2010, she also performed at the Hope for Haiti Now concert, a global benefit for Haitian earthquake relief that also featured stars such as Alicia

Keys, Stevie Wonder, and Shakira. The benefit raised more than $61 million in donations.

In addition, it was during this period that Beyoncé developed themes of female empowerment in her songwriting and performance. Her second album, *B'Day*, was primarily inspired by her role in *Dreamgirls* and by the famous Creole jazz dancer and singer Josephine Baker. In 2006, Beyoncé paid **homage** to the dancer at the Fashion Rocks concert by performing her hit "Déjà Vu" wearing Baker's trademark mini hula skirt adorned with fake bananas. But it was in her songwriting that Beyoncé really began to flex her sociopolitical muscles. Using songs such as "If I Were A Boy," "Irreplaceable," and "Singles Ladies," Beyoncé rewrote the cultural script for women who had been ignored or wronged by romantic partners. R&B traditions of women crying over rejection, such as Etta James's "I Would Rather Go Blind," were blown aside to reveal a stronger, more practical role model of empowered and independent womanhood.

Girl Power

It was not just her parents and upbringing that influenced Beyoncé's music, but the time she grew up in. During the 1990s, a particular movement came to prominence that would hugely influence the entire entertainment industry–the "Girl Power" phenomenon. The Oxford English Dictionary describes "girl power" as "power exercised by girls; a self-reliant attitude among girls and young women manifested in ambition, assertiveness, and individualism."[9] Throughout the 1990s and into the early 2000s, it was a term used to describe female empowerment, independence, and confidence.

The popularity of this message with women led to a huge growth in music, television, and movies featuring strong female characters, such as TV heroine Buffy Summers from *Buffy the Vampire Slayer* and British girl band the Spice Girls. Such women abandoned traditional female roles for more **positive** and empowering ones. *Buffy* made its petite blonde star an action hero rather than a love interest, and the Spice Girls sang about the importance of female friendship rather than crushes and heartbreak. This movement hailed a new era where women were no longer content to see themselves only as damsels in distress, wives, and mothers. They wanted to save themselves and earn their own money, and they wanted to see their own stories and struggles on the big screen.

This message can be seen clearly in the music of Destiny's Child and in Beyoncé's solo work. While she does discuss love and men, she frequently emphasizes the importance of financial and emotional

Sarah Michelle Gellar as the petite, but tough as nails, vampire slayer Buffy Summers

independence, self-reliance, and having control over your own destiny. Beyoncé uses her music to express pride in her femininity. Her songs also highlight how being strong is as much a part of being female as it has traditionally been a part of being male.

CHAPTER FOUR

The Queen Bey

Though Beyoncé's early career has delivered many inspiring anthems, her key contributions to the music industry and the flourishing of her political activism happened after her 2010 career break. It was after this **reflective** pause that her work became more complex, more challenging, and more groundbreaking. After more than a decade working as an entertainer, Beyoncé's work moved to a new level and began not just to reflect modern pop culture but to create it. This change can be documented through her last three albums: *4*, *Beyoncé*, and *Lemonade*.

Beyoncé brings glitz, glamour, and show-stopping power to each of her performances.

The Magic Number

When Beyoncé returned from her year out, she returned in full form. Her comeback single, "Run the World (Girls)," was a confident feminist dance track with a thumping bassline. Everything from its lyrics to its music video worked to create an image of an army ready for battle. She quickly followed this up with the ballad "Best Thing I Never Had," a song that turned a traditional story line—being let down by a lover—into a celebration of escaping a bad relationship. The video features Beyoncé dressed for a wedding to her "true love" and joyfully singing about "dodging a bullet" from her previous bad relationship. The album itself was finally released on June 28, 2011, and it opened at the top of the *Billboard* 200 chart. It sold 310,000 copies in its first week and gave the singer her fourth consecutive number-one album. It included later hits such as "Love on Top," "Party," and "Countdown."

To create the album, Beyoncé went back to her musical roots in traditional R&B and collaborated with songwriters and producers like The-Dream, Tricky Stewart, and Shea Taylor. The goal was to create a mellower tone and use influences from funk, hip-hop, and soul. She moved away somewhat from her usual style of dance songs, like "Crazy in Love" and "Single Ladies." Instead, she wanted to create something more meaningful and intimate. It was from this point that

Beyoncé's work became more open and honest. Its lyrics and subject matter focused on **monogamy**, female empowerment, and self-reflection. She titled the album *4* and would later explain that four was a special number for her. It was the day of her husband and her mother's birthdays, as well as her own, and also the day of her wedding anniversary. The album did well, and at the Fifty-Fifth Annual Grammy Awards, Beyoncé won Best Traditional R&B Performance for "Love on Top."

Knock Out

On December 13, 2013, without announcement or promotion, a brand new Beyoncé album appeared on the iTunes online store. Both Beyoncé's fans and the internet at large were thrown into excitement and confusion. Where had it come from? How had no one known this was coming? Over one million digital copies were purchased in the first six days. The self-titled album, *Beyoncé*, went straight to number one, giving the singer her fifth consecutive number-one album. Two of its tracks, "Drunk in Love" and "***Flawless," would become not only wildly successfully but add new words and phrases into the conversations of millions.

But how and why was the album kept so secret? Beyoncé would later explain that she felt that album releases had lost much of the excitement they used to hold.

The singer at her self-titled album release party in New York City

I miss that immersive experience ... Now people only listen to a few seconds of a song on their iPods and they don't really invest in the whole experience ... I don't want anybody to get the message when my record is coming out. I just want this to come out when it's ready and from me to my fans.[1]

She felt that an album release had essentially lost meaning as a significant event. As a result, through 2013 she worked on the project with a tightly knit group using the code name "Lily." Even within the team, deadlines were constantly shifted and only finalized a week before the album's release. Spokespeople for Beyoncé continued to deny the album's existence right up until its release, stating that once a new album was completed it would be announced via an official press release.

Like its predecessor *4*, *Beyoncé* moved away from the singer's previous pop image to explore darker themes, including body image, depression, and the difficulties of marriage and motherhood. The album was created with an accompanying series of short films, each illustrating the musical concepts Beyoncé wanted to explore.

Even the album's artwork had become more thoughtful and political. Its cover was designed by the album's creative director, Todd Tourso. Inspired by a 1991 Metallica album, Tourso wanted to create something powerful that moved away from the expected "beauty shot" of the singer. He used a font similar to that seen on boxing-match placards,

Beyoncé and Motherhood

On January 7, 2012, Beyoncé gave birth to her first child, Blue Ivy Carter, at Lenox Hill Hospital in New York. Understandably, the event was kept intensely private and was shielded from the press. Both Beyoncé and her husband, Jay Z, were overjoyed at the delivery of a healthy 7-pound (3.2-kilogram) baby and later recorded separate songs about their individual experiences of becoming parents. Beyoncé would eventually describe the moment to magazines as the proudest in her life. Motherhood proved to be yet another field where the singer-actress showed herself to be an inspiration and leader in women's issues.

Juggling a family and a career has long been discussed in the media and in homes across the world. While it is rare that a man's ability to raise a family and succeed in work is questioned, many women have often found their life choices criticized. A woman who works full time while her child is young is often held up as selfish or failing in her "maternal duties." However, Beyoncé continues to show that motherhood and a thriving career are not incompatible.

In 2016, Beyoncé, alongside the British singer Adele, were on the US magazine *Working Mother*'s "Most Powerful Moms" list. The article praised her chart-topping success and business acumen during a period when she was also raising a young child. Sources close to the singer would later reveal in interviews the secret to Beyoncé's work-life balance: timing is key. Since becoming a mother, Beyoncé has placed increased importance on scheduling and time

Beyoncé takes great pride and joy in being a mother to her daughter, Blue Ivy.

frames. Unlike her workaholic past, she now places clear restrictions on rehearsals and meetings. Simply working overtime is no longer an option. She has been known to bring Blue Ivy to rehearsals just to ensure they have more time together.

Beyoncé is lucky enough to be able to manage her schedule and childcare needs with a team of personal assistants and nannies. However, she still places high priority on personal time alone with her family. She proves that with a solid support network, it is possible to have a wildly successful career and a fulfilling family life.

In February 2017, Beyoncé announced via Instagram that she and her husband were expecting twins.

but he contrasted this association by turning the font pink. It gave the image an interesting combination of masculinity and femininity, hinting to listeners how the album would explore what it means to be "feminine."

The album's standout track was undoubtedly "***Flawless," a song about feeling great and not allowing others to make you feel small. Its iconic line "I woke up like this" soon became a popular hashtag on Twitter for girls and guys to celebrate great pictures of themselves. The song also had a strong feminist undercurrent and even explicitly featured part of a speech given by author Chimamanda Ngozi Adichie on how women are often forced to lower their ambitions in order to please men. Beyoncé found the speech browsing YouTube and wanted to use it because she felt like the lines were a call to arms. This song, as well as the entire album, contains a running theme of competition, fighting to win, and trophies.

Beyoncé had previously used many different personas to express different sides of her personality: the aggressive performing Sasha, the soulful Beyoncé, the loved-up Mrs. Carter. However, this album didn't seem to have any defined versions of the singer. She explained:

> I think Beyoncé is Beyoncé, Mrs. Carter is Beyoncé, Sasha Fierce is Beyoncé. And I'm finally at a place where I don't have to separate [them]. It's all pieces of me, and just different elements of a personality of a woman, because we are complicated.[2]

All the hard work Beyoncé and her team put into the album paid off. She made history as the first woman in the *Billboard*'s history to have her first five studio albums debut at number one. Fans and critics alike praised her offering. Rob Sheffield, a writer at *Rolling Stone* magazine, wrote in his review:

> *Beyoncé has delivered countless surprises in her 15 years on top of the music world, but she's never dropped a bombshell like this. The Queen Bey woke the world in the midnight hour with a surprise "visual album"—14 new songs, 17 videos, dropped via iTunes with no warning. The whole project is a celebration of the Beyoncé Philosophy, which basically boils down to the fact that Beyoncé can do anything the hell she wants to.*[3]

Music critics soon noticed other artists adopting similar release strategies, such as Drake, D'Angelo, Azalea Banks, J. Cole, and Kid Cudi.

At the August 2014 MTV Video Music Awards, Beyoncé won Best Video with a Social Message and Best Cinematography for "Pretty Hurts," and Best Collaboration for "Drunk in Love." Later, in February 2015, Beyoncé was nominated for six Grammy Awards and won three, including Best R&B Performance and Best R&B Song for "Drunk in Love," and Best Surround Sound Album for *Beyoncé*.

Making Lemonade

On February 6, 2016, Beyoncé released her brand-new single "Formation." It was immediately obvious from its

The release of "Formation" brought a new tone and energy to Beyoncé's music and political activism.

deep bass and Beyoncé's emphasized use of her Southern accent that she intended to move even further away from her clean-cut "Single Ladies" image. The music video was released exclusively on music streaming platform Tidal and features images of Beyoncé lying on top of a New Orleans police car as it slowly sinks under the waters of a flooded town. An opening voice-over asks, "What happened at the New Orleans?" Most, naturally, took this as a reference to continuing issues over support for Hurricane Katrina victims and as a comment on problems between law enforcement and black communities. Beyoncé was sending a clear message. She was not ashamed of her roots, and she was officially burning her pure pop image. She did not want to be loved by everyone. She was going to be brutally honest with the world, and those who didn't like this new stance could step aside.

She followed one controversial move with another. Performing at the 2016 NFL Super Bowl Halftime Show, Beyoncé dressed her dancers in black with afros and berets, and incorporated raised fists into the dance routine. This was read as a reference to the fiftieth anniversary of the Black Panther Party, a black nationalist organization. It was controversial as the NFL forbids political statements in its performances, but also because Beyoncé had previously avoided discussing race in her musical career. Immediately after the performance, Beyoncé announced The Formation World Tour to promote her upcoming but still mysterious album.

On April 16, 2016, she released a teaser clip for a project titled *Lemonade*. This later turned out to be a one-hour visual album, which aired on HBO exactly one week later. A corresponding album was released on Tidal the same day.

Lemonade debuted, unsurprisingly, at number one in the *Billboard* 200 chart. This groundbreaking achievement made Beyoncé the first entertainer in history to have her first six albums debut atop the chart, breaking a record she had previously tied with rapper DMX in 2013. The album sold 485,000 copies in its first week.

Beyoncé's most musically complex album to date, its songs were a mix of pop, blues, rock, hip-hop, soul, funk, country, gospel, and **trap**, and featured guest vocals from artists such as Kendrick Lamar, The Weeknd, and Jack White. The album's title, *Lemonade*, was inspired by Beyoncé's grandmother Agnez, and also Jay Z's grandmother Hattie White. At the end of track "Freedom," the listener can hear a recording of White speaking at her ninetieth birthday party back in December 2015:

> *I had my ups and downs, but I always find the inner strength to pull myself up. I was served lemons, but I made lemonade.*

The album dealt with issues Beyoncé had experienced in her personal life, but she also tried to make it accessible for all women. Tidal described it as "every woman's journey of self-knowledge and healing."[4] It was widely speculated by both media and public alike that the album was biographical, referring to issues within Beyoncé and Jay Z's marriage and a possible affair between Jay Z and an unnamed woman. The visual album, a sixty-minute film, was first aired on HBO on April 23, 2016. It is divided into titled sections called "Intuition," "Denial," "Anger," "Apathy," "Emptiness," "Accountability," "Reformation," "Forgiveness," "Resurrection," "Hope," and "Redemption." The film follows a storyline of the singer being betrayed and then going through different stages of grief before accepting the betrayal and moving on. It features poetry by Somali poet Warsan Shire, such as "The Unbearable Weight of Staying" and "For Women Who Are Difficult to Love." The film also has guest cameos by famous black women across many different industries, such as tennis player Serena Williams, actress Quvenzhané Wallis, and singer Zendaya. In addition, the visual album makes frequent references to the Black Lives Matter movement and shows the mothers of Trayvon Martin, Michael Brown, and Eric Garner holding pictures of their deceased sons. The film's original broadcast was watched by over 787,000 viewers.

Its reception was stunning. Her most critically acclaimed work to date, the album was almost immediately praised as her boldest and best-crafted work ever. It received a five-star rating from *Rolling Stone* magazine, a rare honor in recent years. The *Lemonade* film was nominated for eleven MTV Video Music awards, the most Beyoncé had ever received. She went on to win eight of her nominations, including Video of the Year for "Formation." These wins secured her place as the most awarded artist in the history of the VMAs, with twenty-four awards. This surpassed previous record holder Madonna and her twenty awards. Beyoncé won five awards at the 2016 BET Awards, receiving Video of the Year, the Centric Award, and the Viewer's Choice Award. The *Lemonade* film itself was nominated for four Primetime Emmy awards, including Outstanding Variety Special and Outstanding Directing for a Variety Special.

Bey Fearless: Dealing with Criticism

Despite her legions of fans, and her infamous online fan group the "BeyHive," Beyoncé has never been without her critics. At many points in her life, the singer has been criticized publicly over her image, her music, her business choices, and her personal life.

At the start of her acting career, she was initially met with skepticism from the press. Many believed she did not have the necessary acting skills to succeed. However, she continued to pursue acting, advancing her skills and working on more and more complex films. By ignoring critics and not shying away from risk, Beyoncé eventually took leading roles in internationally acclaimed films such as *Dreamgirls* and *Cadillac Records*.

After publicly claiming the title of "feminist," Beyoncé has received criticism from feminist scholars arguing that the singer does not promote the "right kind" of feminism. Noted black feminist scholar bell hooks even went so far as to call the singer a "terrorist" because of the way she presented her body in music videos; hooks claimed it set a bad example for young girls. Regardless of whether this is true or not, Beyoncé has continued to judge for herself what makes her a feminist. She is a strong leader because she clearly understands her own beliefs and refuses to allow others to dictate whether those beliefs are right or wrong.

Following the song's release, Beyoncé was criticized over her single "Formation" by outlets such as Fox News. They claimed that the imagery she used was promoting and celebrating "cop killers." In early 2016, former New York City mayor Rudy Giuliani described her Super Bowl performance as "outrageous" and claimed that she had used the show as "a platform to attack police officers," despite the fact it had ended in the crowd spelling out the phrase "Believe in Love!" Beyoncé later countered these claims in an *Elle* magazine interview:

> Anyone who perceives my message as anti-police is completely mistaken. I have so much admiration and respect for officer and the families of officers who sacrifice themselves to keep us safe. But let's be clear: I am against police brutality and injustice. Those are two separate things.

Once again, Beyoncé dealt with criticism like a true leader: honest, direct, but still loyal to her values.

CHAPTER FIVE

Who Run the World?

I t is important to remember that Beyoncé is more than simply her musical career. She is a symbol for female power and an icon for a generation. Her words have weight, and her actions influence millions of people around the globe. As a result, another important aspect of Beyoncé's leadership is her activism. Over the years, she has supported and spoken on behalf of many different causes. However, there are three key issues where she has used her public platform to promote change: feminism, racism, and poverty.

Beyoncé performs "Formation" at the 2016 Super Bowl 50 Halftime Show.

Beyoncé and U2 front man Bono visit the Baphumelele orphanage in South Africa.

Independent Woman Pt. 2

From her early beginnings with Destiny's Child, Beyoncé's music and persona promoted a message of female empowerment, but she never explicitly called herself or her music "feminist." This was fairly standard in the music industry at the time. The label "feminist" had been made into a negative thing. Most people believed it meant a person, usually a woman, who hated men. Worried that the name would not accurately portray their beliefs and alienate their male fans, many female entertainers disowned the "feminist" label in favor and the softer, friendlier "Girl Power" movement of the 1990s. In the words of feminist critic Chimamanda Ngozi Adichie, who Beyoncé would later quote, a feminist is "a person who believes in the social, political, and economic equality of the sexes."[1] Under this definition, Beyoncé's songs have always been feminist. Her music created a space where female problems could be explored and respect could be demanded with the support of a female community. As the singer matured and her political confidence grew, her music not just explored being independent and demanding equality, but also celebrated more traditionally female qualities such as compassion and empathy. Her message was that being emotional could be something powerful rather than a weakness.

Her key feminist moments include the release of her single "***Flawless" and her work with Chime for Change. "***Flawless" was first debuted on the album *Beyoncé*. It was on this album that the singer made her first major steps toward becoming a more political artist. The song itself used sections of a TEDx Talk speech given by Chimamanda Ngozi Adichie titled "We Should All Be Feminists":

As Beyoncé has matured as an artist, her feminist message has grown.

We teach girls to shrink themselves, to make themselves smaller. We say to girls: "You can have ambition, but not too much. You should aim to be successful, but not too successful. Otherwise, you will threaten the man." Because I am female, I am expected to aspire to marriage. I am expected to make my life choices, always keeping in mind that marriage is the most important. Now, marriage can be a source of joy and love and mutual support. But why do we teach girls to aspire to marriage and we don't teach boys the same? We raise girls to see each other as competitors— not for jobs or for accomplishments, which I think can be a good thing, but for the attention of men.[2]

Beyoncé's use of Adichie's words did two things. First, it reframed the song as not just a feel-good anthem but a battle cry against social injustice and forced gender roles. Second, it showed explicitly where Beyoncé's political allegiance lay and encouraged her fans to no longer be afraid to call themselves "feminists." When she performed the song live for the first time, she did so standing proudly in front of a giant fluorescent sign that read "FEMINIST."

Her other key feminism moment was back in 2013 when she joined forces with actress Salma Hayek and Italian fashion designer Frida Giannini to promote Gucci's "Chime for Change" campaign. Launched in February of that year, the campaign's aims were to empower women and girls through education, health and justice. On June 1, a concert for the cause was held in London including other prominent female acts such as Ellie Goulding, Florence and the Machine, and Rita Ora. In the run-up to the event, Beyoncé appeared in a campaign video along with Cameron Diaz, John Legend, and Kylie Minogue. In the video, the celebrities describe how their mothers inspired them. The campaign also asked viewers to submit photos of women who inspired them, and a selection of these were shown at the final concert.

Beyoncé's engagement with feminism and female empowerment has been inspirational for both women who are financially ambitious, and women dealing with day-to-day emotional problems connected with relationships, family, and work. Many writers and media commentators have praised Beyoncé's part in the "resurrection" of feminism, making it once again a rallying cry and not a dirty word.

Unsurprisingly, those who have criticized Beyoncé's brand of feminism have stated that she is both too much and not enough. Earlier in her career, the singer faced criticism from male critics and fans due to songs such as "Bills, Bills, Bills." The idea that a woman would publically criticize a man for constantly borrowing money from his girlfriend was then perceived as excessive and "man-hating." Today, Beyoncé has been more commonly criticized for either not being feminist enough or for using feminism to sell her music. Critics have argued that a woman who uses her looks to sell products, like music, cannot truly be a feminist. It's an interesting argument, but one that ultimately overlooks the empowering effect Beyoncé's music has had on the self-esteem of millions of fans.

#BlackLivesMatter

Before the release of *Beyoncé* and *Lemonade*, Beyoncé generally avoided public discussions of race or racial issues within America. The singer is well known for her premium on privacy, but this silence was possibly enforced through record labels who did not want their artists to be involved in a politically charged dialogue. Since taking over her own management, Beyoncé has spoken more and more openly about celebrating black culture and about issues of police brutality in black communities.

Her involvement in this ongoing issue began publically in 2013, when she and husband Jay Z attended a rally in response to the acquittal of George Zimmerman for the shooting of Trayvon Martin. Later, at the 2015 Grammy Awards, Beyoncé gave a performance of "Take My Hand, Precious Lord." During the routine, dancers held up their hands as if facing a police officer. This symbolic gesture tied the performance to Black Lives Matter, an international activist movement campaigning against violence and systematic racism toward black people. Afterward, she released a

Black Lives Matter demonstrators at the thirtieth annual Martin Luther King Jr. Kingdom Day Parade in Los Angeles

short documentary titled *Take My Hand, Precious Lord: The Voices*. It features interviews with her backup singers discussing the Ferguson riots, Eric Garner, and their experiences of being black in America.

However, Beyoncé's strongest gesture came in the form of her 2016 album *Lemonade*—first, with her single "Formation." and second, with the corresponding video for the track "Freedom." The "Formation" music video makes references to police violence and continuing struggles of black communities affected by Hurricane

Katrina. In the *Lemonade* film, as she performs the song "Freedom," itself an anthem against oppression, the mothers of police brutality victims Trayvon Martin, Michael Brown, and Eric Garner are shown holding photos of their deceased sons. Beyoncé addressed the backlash she had received from some in a rare interview with *Elle* magazine:

> *If celebrating my roots and culture during Black History Month made anyone uncomfortable, those feelings were there long before a video and long before me.*[3]

In the aftermath of the killings of Philando Castile and Alton Sterling, Beyoncé posted a statement on her website:

> *These robberies of lives make us feel helpless and hopeless, but we have to believe that we are fighting for the rights of the next generation, for the next young men and women who believe in good.*[4]

Following this statement, she performed "Freedom" at a concert in Glasgow, sung acappella in front of a screen bearing the names of police brutality victims.

The effect of Beyoncé's increasing participation in this political movement is difficult to show in figures, but it has clearly had an impact. In an online piece by the *New York Times*, it was argued:

> *Beyoncé's activism has been more closely tied to her art. Early this year, she released "Formation," on which she sang intensely about black beauty and cultural pride. In the video, a dancing black boy induces a row of armed officers to raise their hands in surrender, and Beyoncé herself is draped atop a police cruiser as it sinks into the water. Her vigorous Super Bowl halftime show performance of the song included nods to the Black Panthers; it was the most widely seen act of political art in recent memory.*[5]

As well as her cultural statements, both Beyoncé and her husband have donated large sums of money to aid advocacy efforts. On the fourth anniversary of Trayvon Martin's death, the couple donated $1.5 million to several civil right organizations, and through their co-owned music streaming company Tidal, the pair have donated to Black Lives Matter, Hands Up United, and Dream Defenders.

One of the most important aspects of Beyoncé's work has been the way she promotes and shows pride in black culture, black beauty, and her own Southern roots. She has worked hard to give young women, and in particular young black women, positive representations of themselves in the media.

Philanthropy

As a result of her success—and perhaps more importantly, her beliefs—Beyoncé places a great deal of importance on giving back, both to her community and the wider world.

During her time filming *Cadillac Records*, Beyoncé did research into addiction and recovery. Her character, Etta James, was well known for her struggles with alcoholism, and Beyoncé wanted to capture the role realistically. As part of her preparation, the singer visited Phoenix House, a project that helps addicts through the use of medicine, therapy, and social work. She spoke to staff and patients, and her experience stayed with her. During her visit, she noticed that the job training the center provided didn't include beauty therapy. As a result, she donated her entire salary from the film as seed money for the organization to open a cosmetology center. The new venture would train recovering patients to enter a career in hairdressing or beauty treatments, and thus support themselves and find new purpose in something they enjoyed. The aim was to give people the tools to build a new life and a goal to work toward.

In 2013, Beyoncé took the opportunity to start her own philanthropic campaign, the #BeyGood initiative. The aim of the program was to help sick children, the homeless, and the unemployed. However, #BeyGood soon branched out into other areas. In April 2014, Beyoncé contributed to the #BringOurGirlsBack campaign after nearly three hundred schoolgirls were abducted by Boko Haram, an Islamic terrorist organization in Nigeria. Part of the reason for the abduction was that Boko Haram believed girls should not be educated. Their stance created an international discussion on the modern state of women's education. Many barriers remain to education for girls due to the cost of education and long-held cultural beliefs in male superiority and female subordination. Beyoncé encouraged her fans to donate $10 each to Chime for Change projects aiding the education of women in Nigeria.

In May 2015, Beyoncé visited hospitals in Haiti with the #BeyGood initiative and met with thousands of sick children. She did this primarily to show support for victims of the 2010 earthquake and to raise awareness of ongoing efforts to repair the damage. In 2016, at the start of her Formation World Tour, she announced the initiative's intention to partner with the United Water Way to offer aid to those affected by the water crisis in Flint, Michigan. This was in addition to partnering with Chime for Change and Global Citizen. Another of Beyoncé's personal projects was the Survivor Foundation, an organization she founded with Kelly Rowland to help victims of Hurricane Katrina. One of the foundation's biggest accomplishments was the creation of the Music World Cares Christmas Carnival. This event was designed to give over three hundred low-income households a fun-filled day of food, entertainment, visits from Santa Claus, and free toys from the giveaway.

Children's causes have long held a special place for Beyoncé. Back in 2005, she was asked to be a World Children's Day ambassador. As part of the campaign, she released the single "Stand Up for Love" with fellow Destiny's Child members Kelly Rowland and Michelle Williams. The song was released globally on November 20 to raise awareness and funds for children's charities and organizations.

While no stranger to the limelight, Beyoncé has also shown herself to be equally generous in private. After two of her fans were injured by a fireworks accident at her concert, she discreetly visited the hospital shortly after the concert ended. The head nurse on duty later revealed:

She was just very concerned about the people injured in the audience. It was unannounced and we kept it very low-key so that she could spend time with them.[6]

In total, Beyoncé publically supports over thirty charities and foundations. She has actively used her success to help give back and support causes she believes in. She also encourages philanthropy among her fans, such as requesting them to bring old, unwanted clothes to concerts as a charity donation.

Why is "Formation" Political?

We all know that when we read a book or watch a film, that there are different ways to tell a story. If we are reading a book, we of course have words, but sometimes there are also pictures. These pictures can add to or change the meaning of those words. Similarly, when we watch a film, we are not just listening to what the actors say. We are looking at the colors the director uses, the choice of setting, the props the actors hold or ignore. The same can be applied to songs and their accompanying videos. Why is the singer or director showing us a particular image? What does it mean? How do they want us to feel? What do they want us to think about? This makes music videos extremely powerful for delivering political messages or protests.

"Formation" uses two particular kinds of imagery. First, it invokes things traditionally associated with black Southern culture. The voice-over talks about "cornbread and collard greens" as we see black women dressed in antebellum dresses and Beyoncé outfitted in a New Orleans–inspired carnival costume. Through her lyrics and her poses on-screen, she exudes confidence and pride. For hundreds of years, black culture has been largely ignored or appropriated by mainstream white culture. Beyoncé references this by showing images from the past (antebellum America) and present day (the New Orleans Carnival) to show how far black rights have come. She is trying to show both pride and ownership of her heritage and culture.

Second, the video features images that address the Black Lives Matter movement, such as a young black boy dancing in front of riot police, and a spray-painted wall that reads "Stop Shooting Us." Beyoncé's use of these images forces the watcher to acknowledge the movement and its message, bringing the discussion of police brutality and racial injustice into mainstream conversation.

Sometimes, if we don't understand the references we are being shown, it is easy to dismiss the message in a music video. However, it is important to remember that different images can mean different things to different people. Beyoncé has used images that she knows will send a message to certain people, specifically black communities who feel a connection with either the South or the Black Lives Matter movement.

CHAPTER SIX

Keep Running

Beyoncé has spent nearly three decades of her life in the public eye, from her early years taking dance classes, singing in choirs, and entering beauty pageants, to her more recent ventures into visual albums and politically charged musical statements. She is someone who leads by example, constantly pushing and shaping herself to be successful in what most inspires her and also frequently looking to break new ground. Her success is self-evident. There are very few people in the Western world who do not know her name, and she has millions of fans abroad. In addition, as a solo artist she

Beyoncé greets fans outside the 2014 MTV Video Music Awards.

has sold over sixteen million albums in the United States and over one hundred million worldwide. Paired with the sixty million albums she sold as a member of Destiny's Child, Beyoncé is one of the best-selling artists of all time—not female artist, but artist period.

Awards and Recognition

Looking back to the beginning of her solo career, it was the lead single "Crazy in Love" from her debut album, *Dangerously in Love*, that truly launched her as an international star. Not only was the song wildly successful but it also received critical acclaim. The track was named VH1's "Greatest Song of the 2000s." *Rolling Stone* magazine placed it on its list of the "500 Greatest Songs of All Time." It earned two Grammy Awards and is still one of the best-selling singles of all time, with around eight million copies sold worldwide.

As she moved forward in her career, Beyoncé continued to garner awards for her work. In 2006, following her performance in *Dreamgirls*, she won two awards at the Broadcast Film Critics Association Awards: Best Song for "Listen," and Best Original Soundtrack for *Dreamgirls: Music from the Motion Picture*. The following year she was nominated for Best Original Song for "Listen" and Best Actress at the Golden Globes. In 2008, Beyoncé received the Legend Award at the World Music Awards, an international awards show that celebrates outstanding achievements in the record industry.

It was in 2007 that critics began to realize the power and influence that Beyoncé's music and image truly had. The singer received the International Artist of Excellence Award at the American Music Awards. Previous winners of this award include Michael Jackson and Led Zeppelin. At the time, Beyoncé was the only woman to ever receive the award. In 2009 the British newspaper the *Observer* named her Artist of the Decade, and *Billboard* named her both Top Female Artist and Top Radio Songs Artist of the Decade. The following year, *Billboard* also placed her at number fifteen in their "Top 50 R&B/Hip-Hop Artists of the Past 25 Years," and she received the Billboard Millennium Award at the Billboard Music Awards in 2011. One year before her influential *Beyoncé* album dropped, VH1 ranked her third on their list of the "100 Greatest Women in Music."

In 2013, her influence was even further acknowledged when Beyoncé was included on the *Time* 100 list. This is an annual list published by *Time* magazine that ranks the hundred most influential people in the world. In 2014, after the release of *Beyoncé*, she appeared on the list again, and this time she was the featured cover model. Her profile, by technology executive, writer, and activist Sheryl Sandberg, described Beyoncé as someone who "doesn't just sit at the table. She builds a better one."[1] The same year, she was honored with the Michael Jackson Video Vanguard Award at the 2014 MTV Video Music Awards. In 2016, she received the Fashion Icon Award at the CFDA Fashion Awards.

As well as her many awards, Beyoncé has also received frequent recognition from a number of major bodies. The Recording Industry Association of America listed the singer as the Top Certified Artist of the 2000s with a total of over sixty different certifications. Certifications are awarded when large numbers of an album or single are sold. Gold awards are given when five hundred thousand copies are sold, platinum awards are when one million copies are sold, and multi-platinum is when over two million copies are sold. The highest award is diamond certification for when an artist sells ten million copies. Currently "Single Ladies (Put A Ring On It)," "Irreplaceable," and "Halo" are ranked multi-platinum and are among the best-selling records of all time.

Beyoncé has received many honors and nominations from the Grammy Awards, both as a solo artist and as part of Destiny's Child. She has so far won twenty awards, making her the second most honored female artist in Grammy Award history, just behind Alison Krauss. With fifty-two nominations, Beyoncé is the most-nominated woman in Grammy Award history, In 2010, her smash hit "Single Ladies (Put A Ring On It)" won Song of the Year. That year, she set the record for the most Grammy Awards won by a female artist in a single night, breaking her previous tie with Norah Jones, Alison Krauss, Amy Winehouse, and Alicia Keys. She was equaled by British singer Adele in 2012. Her albums

Dangerously in Love, B'Day, and *I Am … Sasha Fierce*
have all won the Best Contemporary R&B Album award.

MTV has also given much recognition to Beyoncé's
efforts over the years. To date, the signer has won twenty-
four MTV awards, making her the most awarded artist
in MTV history. She has won Video of the Year twice,
with "Single Ladies (Put A Ring On It)" in 2009 and
"Formation" in 2016. At the 2016 MTV Video Music
Awards, she tied the record previously held by singer
Lady Gaga for most VMAs won in a single night by a
female artist, with eight awards.

Legacy

Though awards are important for recognizing the
contributions an artist has made to the world, they are
not our only way to determine the effect artists have had
on our lives. The legacies they create and help form the
world we live in and the culture that surrounds us. So
what kind of legacy has Beyoncé created?

First, she is a groundbreaker. She is a hugely
successfully and powerful artist in an industry where
the majority of power and influence still lies with male
artists, producers, and record company executives. She
established her own entertainment and management
company, Parkwood Entertainment, which develops
products for music, film, and television. The company
has also collaborated on fashion projects with British
retailer Topshop. Through this venture, Beyoncé was able

to not only take control of her own management but also assist and produce younger artists. Her incredible work ethic and output has contributed to her rise in fame and respect. Currently she is ranked third on the Harris Interactive Poll of America's Favorite Musical Artist of All Time, after the Beatles and Elvis Presley. In July 2014, the Rock and Roll Hall of Fame expanded its Legends of Rock section to include a special Beyoncé exhibit honoring her contributions to music history. Among the pieces included where her black leotard from the "Single Ladies (Put A Ring On It)" video and the outfit from her 2013 Super Bowl halftime performance.

Second, she commands respect and admiration from both critics and industry professionals alike. In the *New Yorker* magazine, music critic Jody Rosen described the singer as "the most important and compelling popular musician of the twenty-first century ... the result, the logical end point, of a century-plus of pop."[2]

British newspaper the *Guardian* wrote a piece on Beyoncé after naming her Artist of the Decade, declaring:

Why Beyoncé? ... Because she made not one but two of the decade's greatest singles, with "Crazy in Love" and "Single Ladies (Put a Ring on It)," not to mention her hits with Destiny's Child; and this was the decade when singles— particularly R&B singles—regained their status as pop's favorite medium ... She and not any superannuated rock star was arguably the greatest live performer of the past 10 years.[3]

After she made the *Time* 100 list in 2013, director Baz Luhrmann wrote:

> *No one has that voice, no one moves the way she moves, no one can hold an audience the way she does ... When Beyoncé does an album, when Beyoncé sings a song, when Beyoncé does anything, it's an event, and it's broadly influential. Right now, she is the heir-apparent diva of the USA—the reigning national voice.*[4]

Third, her stylistic choices in music videos, performances, and even song lyrics have greatly influenced culture. Her music video for "Single Ladies (Put A Ring On It)" spawned thousands of copies in part due to the intricate dance routine and in part due to the catchy phrase "Put a ring on it." Soon enough, the line was appearing over all the internet and was even quoted in television series and films. The song was credited as starting the first dance craze of the internet age. Similarly, songs like "***Flawless" sparked millions of Twitter hashtags, Tumblr memes, and branded accessories with phrases such as "#Flawless" and "I woke up like this," creating a new language of confidence and self-celebration.

Fourth, Beyoncé has been and continues to be a huge inspiration to other artists. Performers who have referenced her as an influence include Adele, Ariana Grande, Lady Gaga, Ellie Goulding, Rihanna, Sam Smith, Meghan Trainor, Grimes, Rita Ora, Azealia Banks, and

Beyoncé's "Single Ladies" routine is now notorious across the internet and modern pop culture.

many more. She is often referenced in songs by female artists as an object of inspiration, and by male artists as an object of attraction. Some artists have even used her work directly. For example, in 2013 the Canadian rapper Drake released the track "Girls Love Beyoncé" which references the chorus of the Destiny's Child track "Say My Name." The track discussed his relationships with women, with frequent references to how many girls were inspired by Beyoncé's image of strength and independence.

Future Plans

Silence and secrecy have been Beyoncé's watchwords for several years now. Since taking over her own management, she has given fewer interviews and instead chosen careful and constructive ways to give out information to her fans, such as through social media or through the imagery and messages of her music. This is actually a very clever strategy on her part and has a number of consequences. It makes the information she does release seem more interesting and exciting because the public has become used to her being heavily guarded about her information. Furthermore, there is less opportunity to spoil or overshadow her musical image through a misunderstood or misquoted comment to a reporter. In addition, her secrecy always keeps people curious and guessing what her next move might be. Without trying, Beyoncé keeps herself relevant and interesting as people try to speculate on what to expect from her next. Lastly, when she does release an album or single, the lack of previous information means that a Beyoncé release causes instant excitement and turns a simple release into a major cultural event. Fans and critics immediately take to social media to announce the arrival, talk show hosts will publicize the event and the meaning of its timing, and immediately the internet is drawn into an analysis of its meaning and content.

Though sources are vague, there are some clues as to what the entertainment mogul will be up to in the next few years. It is believed that she will be releasing a joint visual album with her husband, Jay Z, as well as planning another worldwide tour at the end of 2017. She has dropped hints that she would like to do more directing and work more behind the camera. This desire seems to match up to her more recent desires to find and develop new talent. For example, she has signed YouTube singing duo Chloe x Halle under Parkwood Entertainment.

Leaving Her Mark

In a 2012 article from business insider *Forbes* magazine, writer Tanya Prive listed the ten most important qualities to be a good leader: honesty, **delegation**, **communication**, confidence, commitment, a positive attitude, creativity, **intuition**, inspiration, and approach.[5] When examining Beyoncé's career, examples of these qualities can be readily found.

Honesty: As Beyoncé has matured and grown more confident in her ethical message, her willingness to engage with important ethical issues has grown greatly. Her music shows two sides of herself. One is the passionate advocate for political and social issues that many people continue to struggle with. The other side is the emotional honesty of her music. Fans and critics connect with her songs because she is able to tap into deep reserves of emotion and be that anger, betrayal, or inspiration.

Delegation: Though Beyoncé sometimes seems to be a one-woman squad, she actually surrounds herself with a strong, highly talented team. While she holds the ultimate creative vision, she makes sure to bring in creative and innovative people to generate and develop the best ideas possible. By working with others, she is able to reap the benefits of other visions and opinions.

Communication: As previously mentioned, Beyoncé is a master of communication. She knows just what to release and when to ensure maximum impact. She doesn't get involved with social media arguments, she doesn't give out personal statements over social media, and she will drop albums with no press release. At the same time, she keeps a close relationship with her fans by providing them with a stream of personal photos and videos that give an insight into her personal life without ever letting the viewer inside completely.

Confidence: Beyoncé approaches all things with confidence. She is a fantastic performer who understands that many of her fans listen to her music for the confidence it gives them. She plays to that image and works to try new things and not fear mistakes.

Commitment: No one would argue Beyoncé's commitment to the entertainment industry. She is clearly in a career she loves, and her work exudes that feeling. It is this commitment that honed her skills in her younger years and has ensured her a reigning place in the music industry and modern culture. Though the media often portrays her life as extremely glamorous, behind the scenes

Beyoncé puts in a lot of time and hard work to ensure that she remains current and continues to grow and evolve.

A Positive Attitude: Beyoncé almost never complains publicly. In interviews and documentaries she is also shown as hard working and gracious. She understands completely how special her life is and how this depends on her own attitude.

Creativity: The singer has always been known for her willingness to try new things. However, it is in her most recent solo work that she has shown her ability to grow and experiment. Beyoncé never rests on what is comfortable or popular, and always pushes herself into new genres, new beats, and new imagery. This has also resulted in exciting new methods for album releases, choreography, and charity functions.

Intuition: As a leader, Beyoncé has learned to trust her instincts. A frequent trailblazer, the singer has never shown interest in following in the footsteps of another star. She is shaping her own significant style and image. This takes a certain amount of foresight to plan how the public might react and also to estimate how successful different ventures might be. Every new project she takes on requires Beyoncé to map out how she wants the project to look upon completion and to plan how she can sell it to the world.

Inspiration: Time and time again, the entertainment mogul has shown herself to be an incredible source of inspiration. Her work ethic, her talent, and her creativity continue to enthuse both fans and critics. Many current artists cite her among their inspirations and influences.

Approach: Successful leaders do not follow tried-and-tested approaches. They look for ways to innovate and new ways to succeed. As has been shown, Beyoncé has developed her own unique method for communication, for the release of her music, and for her own management. She has set the standard for the music industry, and in particular for female artists who have been traditionally controlled by male managers and record company executives.

In the years to come, we expect great things from Beyoncé. In her single "Freedom," she told the world, "Imma keep running, / Cos' a winner don't quit on themselves." To date, her actions have echoed this message. As a leader, she continues to forge a path for women both in the entertainment industry and the rest of the world. She is an inspirational example of a strong, talented, independent woman who has built her career from the ground up. The world waits to see where she will lead us next.

Business Lessons from Beyoncé

Beyoncé isn't just an artistic or cultural leader, she is also a savvy businesswoman. Through talent, hard work, and creativity, she has built an empire that offers her both different outlets to express herself and multiple opportunities for income. These opportunities include endorsements, business ventures, influential friends, awards, albums, and tours.

The singer has garnered many endorsements with popular brands. Examples include L'Oréal, American Express, Tommy Hilfiger, and Emporio Armani. One of her most lucrative deals is a $50 million contract with the soft drink giant Pepsi.

Most of Beyoncé's business ventures have played to the singer's beauty and her carefully crafted image. Back in 2005, she set up the House of Deréon with her mother, Tina, in honor of her maternal grandmother. The lines were initially presented at Destiny's Child concerts and were later available in selected stores across America. In 2007, Beyoncé began one of her biggest ventures yet with the establishment of her own entertainment and management company, Parkwood Entertainment. Headquartered in New York City, the company handles all products relating to Beyoncé, including tours, music, and merchandise. Between 2010 and 2013, she released her own line of six different perfumes, with sales of over $400 million. A year later, the singer-turned-mogul teamed up with British fashion retailer Topshop to create Parkwood Topshop Athletic Ltd. The line, known as "Ivy Park," was released in 2016 and contained a selection of different dance, fitness, and sports clothing. In 2015, she became a co-owner of her husband Jay Z's music streaming platform, Tidal.

In addition to selling products, Beyoncé also has a network of influential friends that she can tap into. For example, the singer counts among her friends President Barack Obama and his wife, Michelle. She performed at both the 2008 and 2012 presidential inaugurations, and she held a joint fundraiser with Jay Z for the 2012 Obama presidential campaign.

As already mentioned, Beyoncé has won a huge number of awards and this furthers her empire. She is able to command more money and respect for her work. She is offered more roles in future productions. Her star power continues to rise, and she can use this as a negotiation tactic in business deals.

This same rule applies to her music and tours. Beyoncé's music is her main source of income, but it also aids her other ventures. When her now notorious self-titled album dropped without any previous promotion, it became the fastest-selling album of all time. Businesses know that Beyoncé is a shrewd marketer who knows how to excite her public. While the album sales all add to her paycheck, they also encourage companies to offer her the best endorsement deals possible. They know Beyoncé's face will help sell their product, and Beyoncé can leverage that power to her own advantage.

Timeline

2001

Destiny's Child releases third studio album, *Survivor*.

2006

Beyoncé's second solo album, *B'Day*, is released. Musical film *Dreamgirls* premieres.

1997

Destiny's Child releases their first hit single, "No, No, No."

2003

Launch of debut solo album, *Dangerously in Love*, including single "Crazy in Love."

Destiny's Child releases self-titled debut album.

1998

Destiny's Child releases final studio album, *Destiny Fulfilled*.

2004

Beyoncé Giselle Knowles is born in Houston, Texas.

1981

Beyoncé releases first solo single, "Work It Out." She features on the single "'03 Bonnie & Clyde" with Jay Z.

2002

2010

Beyoncé decides to take a nine-month hiatus from her music career. She wins six awards in one night at the Fifty-Second Grammy Awards.

2013

Release of fifth studio album, *Beyoncé*, with no previous announcement or promotion.

2011

Release of fourth album, *4*. Becomes the first solo female artist to headline the main Pyramid Stage at Glastonbury Festival.

Jay Z and Beyoncé marry in a private ceremony in New York City. Beyoncé releases "Single Ladies (Put A Ring On It)" and her third studio album, *I Am … Sasha Fierce*. *Cadillac Records* is released.

Birth of Beyoncé's first child, daughter Blue Ivy Carter.

2012

2008

Performs new single "Formation" at the NFL Super Bowl Fifty Halftime Show. Releases sixth album as a one-hour movie entitled *Lemonade* premiering on HBO. Becomes the first woman in history to have her first six solo albums debut at number one on the *Billboard* chart.

2016

SOURCE NOTES

Chapter 1

1. Randy J. Taraborrelli, *Becoming Beyoncé: The Untold Story* (New York: Grand Central Publishing, 2015), 11.

2. Ibid., 18.

3. Ibid., 30.

4. Ibid., 32.

5. Ibid., 14.

6. Ibid., 21.

7. Ibid., 32.

8. Ibid., 33.

Chapter 2

1. Janice Arenofsky, *Beyoncé Knowles: A Biography* (Westport, CT: Greenwood Press, 2009), 31.

2. Ibid., 29.

3. Ibid., 33.

4. Ibid., 35.

5. Gil Kaufman, "Destiny's Child Announce Split," MTV News, June 12, 2005, http://www.mtv.com/news/1503975/destinys-child-announce-split.

Chapter 3

1. Beyoncé Knowles, Kelendria Rowland, and Michelle Williams, *Soul Survivors: The Official Autobiography of Destiny's Child* (New York: HarperCollins, 2002), 150.

2. Daryl Easlea, *Crazy in Love: The Beyoncé Knowles Biography* (London, UK: Omnibus Press, 2014), 13.

3. Ibid., 102.

4. Trish Crawford, "Beyonce's Single an Anthem for Women," *Toronto Star*, January 23, 2009, http://www.thestar.com/ life/2009/01/23/beyonces_single_an_anthem_for_women. html.

5. Jayson Rodriguez, "Kanye West Crashes VMA Stage During Taylor Swift's Award Speech," MTV News, September 13, 2009, http://www.mtv.com/news/1621389/kanye-west-crashes-vma-stage-during-taylor-swifts-award-speech.

6. Kevin O'Keeffe, "Taylor Swift Owes Her Career to Beyoncé Thanks to This Classic VMAs Moment," *Mic*, August 28, 2015, https://mic.com/articles/124486/taylor-swift-owes-her-career-to-beyonc-thanks-to-this-classic-vmas-moment#. MKYoQcIUQ.

7. Michael A. Schuman, *Beyoncé: A Biography of a Legendary Singer* (Berkeley Heights, NJ: Enslow Publishers, 2014), 89.

8. Ibid., 89.

9. "Girl Power, n," OED Online, September 2016, http:// dictionary.oed.com.

Chapter 4

1. Taraborrelli, *Becoming Beyoncé*, 415.

2. Kia Makarechi, "Beyoncé Explains the Birth of 'Yoncé' and Breaking 'The Fourth Wall,'" *Huffington Post*, December 21, 2013, http://www.huffingtonpost.com/2013/12/21/beyonce-yonce-screening_n_4487104.html.

3. Rob Sheffield, review of *Beyoncé*, by Beyoncé Knowles, *Rolling Stone*, December 14, 2013, http://www.rollingstone.com/music/albumreviews/beyonce-20131214.

4. Joe Coscarelli, "Beyoncé Releases Surprise Album 'Lemonade' After HBO Special," *New York Times*, April 23, 2016, http://www.nytimes.com/2016/04/24/arts/music/beyonce-hbo-lemonade.html?_r=0.

5. Niraj Chokshi, "Rudy Giuliani: Beyoncé's Halftime Show Was an 'Outrageous' Affront to Police," *Washington Post*, February 8, 2016, https://www.washingtonpost.com/news/arts-and-entertainment/wp/2016/02/08/rudy-giuliani-beyonces-half-time-show-was-an-outrageous-affront-to-police/?utm_term=.6b2eed0f91b5.

6. Eliana Dockterman, "Beyoncé: 'Anyone Who Perceives My Message as Anti-Police Is Completely Mistaken,'" *Time*, April 5, 2016, http://time.com/4282452/beyonce-anyone-who-perceives-my-message-as-anti-police-is-completely-mistaken.

Chapter 5

1. Rhonesha Byng, "WATCH: We Should All Be Feminists: 'We Teach Girls to Shrink Themselves, to Make Themselves Smaller,'" *Her Agenda*, December 14, 2013, http://heragenda.com/watch-we-should-all-be-feminists-we-teach-girls-to-shrink-themselves-to-make-themselves-smaller.

2. Tamar Gottesman, "EXCLUSIVE: Beyoncé Wants to Change the Conversation," *Elle*, April 4, 2016, http://www.elle.com/fashion/a35286/beyonce-elle-cover-photos.

3. Randall Roberts. "Read Beyonce's Open Letter in Response to the Deaths of Alton Sterling and Philando Castile," *Los Angeles Times*, July 7, 2016, http://www.latimes.com/entertainment/music/la-et-ms-beyonce-open-letter-sterling-castile-20160707-snap-story.html.

4. Jon Caramanica, "Jay Z and Beyoncé: Activism Gone Vocal," *New York Times*, July 8, 2016, http://www.nytimes.com/2016/07/09/arts/music/beyonce-jay-z-police-killings-spiritual.html.

5. "Beyoncé Visits Fans in Hospital," BBC News, July 10, 2007, http://news.bbc.co.uk/2/hi/entertainment/6287000.stm.

Chapter 6

1. Sheryl Sandberg, "Beyoncé," *Time*, April 23, 2014, http://time.com/70716.

2. Jody Rosen, "Her Highness," *New Yorker*, February 20, 2013, http://www.newyorker.com/culture/culture-desk/her-highness.

3. Caspar Llewellyn Smith, "Beyoncé: Artist of the Decade," *Guardian*, November 28, 2009, https://www.theguardian.com/music/2009/nov/29/beyonce-artist-of-the-decade.

4. Baz Luhrmann, "Beyoncé: Diva, 31," *Time*, April 18, 2013, http://time100.time.com/2013/04/18/time-100/slide/beyonce.

5. Tanya Prive, "Top 10 Qualities That Make a Great Leader," *Forbes*, December 19, 2012, http://www.forbes.com/sites/tanyaprive/2012/12/19/top-10-qualities-that-make-a-great-leader/#2c8d44603564.

GLOSSARY

approach The method used in setting about a task or problem.

attitude A person's manner or feeling towards another person or thing.

branding Giving a company or figure a particular image in order to advertise its products and services.

commitment Making a promise to do something and sticking to it.

communication The giving and receiving of thoughts, opinions, or information.

concept A principle or idea.

confidence The feeling or belief that one can rely on someone or something; firm trust.

creativity Ability to think outside of traditional patterns and rules to create meaningful new ideas.

Creole Someone who is related to the first Europeans who came to the Caribbean or the southern United States.

delegation To give power or assign work to another person.

emotional range Ability to display or feel a number of different emotions.

empowered Having the authority or freedom to do something.

foray A period of time being involved in an activity that is different from usual activities.

homage The act of showing respect and admiration to a person or their memory.

honesty The act of being truthful and fair.

inspiration To make others feel capable of achieving great things or to influence people to create new things.

intuition Quick and keen insight, or good instincts.

jargon Special words and phrases used by a particular group of people.

mainstream Considered normal and accepted by most people.

monogamy The custom of being faithful to only one person at a time.

multidimensional Having many different features.

naïveté Trust based on not having much experience.

panned Criticized severely.

persona A character or personality that a person is adopting for a story.

positive Something that is hopeful and confident.

reflective Thinking carefully and quietly.

trap A subgenre of hip-hop music that originated in the Southern United States during the 1990s.

FURTHER INFORMATION

Books

Moore, Madison. *How to Be Beyoncé*. Brooklyn, NY: Thought Catalogue, 2013.

Schuman, Michael A. *Beyoncé: A Biography of a Legendary Singer*. Berkeley Heights, NJ: Enslow Publishers, 2014.

Trier-Bieniek, Adrienne, ed. *The Beyoncé Effect: Essays on Sexuality, Race and Feminism*. Jefferson, NC: McFarland, 2016.

Websites

Beyoncé
http://www.beyonce.com

The singer's official website offers further information about her music, tours, #BeyGood initiative, and more.

HBO Documentaries: Beyoncé
http://www.hbo.com/documentaries/beyonce

Learn more about the singer's career with films and videos from HBO.

New York Times: **Beyoncé**

http://www.nytimes.com/topic/person/beyonce-knowles

Collected *New York Times* articles on Beyoncé's career and cultural presence.

Video

The Year of 4

www.youtube.com/watch?v=3vXXiku0580

This documentary, featuring an interview with Beyoncé, takes a behind-the-scenes look at her year's break from music and the creation of her comeback album, *4*.

BIBLIOGRAPHY

Arenofsky, Janice. *Beyoncé Knowles: A Biography*. Westport, CT: Greenwood Press, 2009

"Beyoncé Visits Fans in Hospital." BBC News, July 10, 2007. http://news.bbc.co.uk/2/hi/entertainment/6287000.stm.

Byng, Rhonesha. "WATCH: We Should All Be Feminists: 'We Teach Girls to Shrink Themselves, to Make Themselves Smaller.'" *Her Agenda*, December 14, 2013. http://heragenda.com/watch-we-should-all-be-feminists-we-teach-girls-to-shrink-themselves-to-make-themselves-smaller.

Caramanica, Jon. "Jay Z and Beyoncé: Activism Gone Vocal." *New York Times*, July 8, 2016. http://www.nytimes.com/2016/07/09/arts/music/beyonce-jay-z-police-killings-spiritual.html.

Chokshi, Niraj. "Rudy Giuliani: Beyoncé's Halftime Show Was an 'Outrageous' Affront to Police." *Washington Post*, February 8, 2016. https://www.washingtonpost.com/news/arts-and-entertainment/wp/2016/02/08/rudy-giuliani-beyonces-half-time-show-was-an-outrageous-affront-to-police/?utm_term=.6b2eed0f91b5.

Coscarelli, Joe. "Beyoncé Releases Surprise Album 'Lemonade' After HBO Special." *New York Times*, April 23, 2016. http://www.nytimes.com/2016/04/24/arts/music/beyonce-hbo-lemonade.html?_r=0.

Crawford, Trish. "Beyonce's Single an Anthem for Women." *Toronto Star*, January 23, 2009. http://www.thestar.com/

life/2009/01/23/beyonces_single_an_anthem_for_women.
html.

Dockterman, Eliana. "Beyoncé: 'Anyone Who Perceives My
Message as Anti-Police Is Completely Mistaken,'" *Time*,
April 5, 2016. http://time.com/4282452/beyonce-anyone-
who-perceives-my-message-as-anti-police-is-completely-
mistaken.

Easlea, Daryl. *Crazy in Love: The Beyoncé Knowles Biography*.
London, UK: Omnibus Press, 2014.

Ellen, Barbara. "Beyoncé: The Superstar Who Brought Black
Power to the Super Bowl." *Guardian*, February 13, 2016.
https://www.theguardian.com/music/2016/feb/14/beyonce-
profile-black-power-super-bowl-civil-rights.

Gottesman, Tamar. "EXCLUSIVE: Beyoncé Wants to Change
the Conversation." *Elle*, April 4, 2016. http://www.elle.com/
fashion/a35286/beyonce-elle-cover-photos.

Hill, Z. B. *Beyoncé*. Superstars of Hip-Hop. Bromall, PA: Mason
Crest, 2013.

Kaufman, Gil. "Destiny's Child Announce Split." MTV News,
June 12, 2005. http://www.mtv.com/news/1503975/destinys-
child-announce-split.

Knowles, Beyonce, Kelendria Rowland, and Michelle Williams.
Soul Survivors: The Official Autobiography of Destiny's Child.
New York: HarperCollins, 2002.

Luhrmann, Baz. "Beyoncé: Diva, 31." *Time*, April 18, 2013. http://
time100.time.com/2013/04/18/time-100/slide/beyonce.

Makarechi, Kia. "Beyoncé Explains the Birth of 'Yoncé' and
Breaking 'The Fourth Wall.'" *Huffington Post*, December 21,
2013. http://www.huffingtonpost.com/2013/12/21/beyonce-
yonce-screening_n_4487104.html.

O'Keeffe, Kevin. "Taylor Swift Owes Her Career to Beyoncé Thanks to This Classic VMAs Moment." *Mic*, August 28, 2015. https://mic.com/articles/124486/taylor-swift-owes-her-career-to-beyonc-thanks-to-this-classic-vmas-moment#.MKYoQcIUQ.

Pointer, Anna. *Beyoncé: Running the World*. London, UK: Hodder and Stroughton, 2014.

Prive, Tanya. "Top 10 Qualities That Make a Great Leader." *Forbes*, December 19, 2012. http://www.forbes.com/sites/tanyaprive/2012/12/19/top-10-qualities-that-make-a-great-leader/#2c8d44603564.

Roberts, Randall. "Read Beyonce's Open Letter in Response to the Deaths of Alton Sterling and Philando Castile." *Los Angeles Times*, July 7, 2016. http://www.latimes.com/entertainment/music/la-et-ms-beyonce-open-letter-sterling-castile-20160707-snap-story.html.

Rodriguez, Jayson. "Kanye West Crashes VMA Stage During Taylor Swift's Award Speech." MTV News, September 13, 2009. http://www.mtv.com/news/1621389/kanye-west-crashes-vma-stage-during-taylor-swifts-award-speech.

Rosen, Jody. "Her Highness." *New Yorker*, February 20, 2013. http://www.newyorker.com/culture/culture-desk/her-highness.

Sandberg, Sheryl. "Beyoncé." *Time*, April 23, 2014. http://time.com/70716.

Schuman, Michael A. *Beyoncé: A Biography of a Legendary Singer*. Berkeley Heights, NJ: Enslow Publishers, 2014.

Sheffield, Rob. Review of *Beyoncé*, by Beyoncé Knowles. *Rolling Stone*, December 14, 2013. http://www.rollingstone.com/music/albumreviews/beyonce-20131214.

Smith, Caspar Llewellyn. "Beyoncé: Artist of the Decade." *Guardian*, November 28, 2009. https://www.theguardian.com/music/2009/nov/29/beyonce-artist-of-the-decade.

Taraborrelli, J. Randy. *Becoming Beyoncé: The Untold Story.* New York: Grand Central Publishing, 2015.

INDEX

ABOUT THE AUTHOR

Katie Griffiths is a long-time lover of music and pop culture from around the world. Her love of different cultures and their stories has taken her to many countries, including China, Japan, and Cambodia. She currently lives in Edinburgh, Scotland. She loves traveling, hiking, and collecting graphic novels in her free time. To learn more and see her other works, visit http://www.katiegriffiths.org.